Inventing what we need to know

poems

W.H. New

Rock's Mills Press
Rock's Mills, Ontario • Oakville, Ontario
2025

Published by
Rock's Mills Press
www.rocksmillspress.com

Copyright © 2025 by W.H. New
All rights reserved. No part of this publication may be reproduced, distributed, or transmitted in any form or by any means, including photocopying, recording, or other electronic or mechanical methods, without the prior written permission of the publisher, except in the case of brief quotations embodied in critical reviews and certain other noncommercial uses permitted by copyright law. For permission requests, contact the publisher at: customer.service@rocksmillspress.com

For adoption, trade, and bulk orders, contact the publisher at:
customer.service@rocksmillspress.com

Rock's Mills Press (both the name and the styling in Rockwell Bold) is a registered trademark and is used under license.

Library and Archives Canada Cataloguing in Publication data has been applied for.

To the memory of Peggy New

Contents

1.
Roots | 8

2.
On fields beside the moon | 11
Harry's brothers | 12
Cables | 13
Fortune-tellers | 14
Filaments | 16
Tin box | 17
Ghosts | 19

3.
Pond ice | 21
Wagon | 22
Biking with shadows | 23
Flood | 24
The cost of land | 25
The field | 26
Riverstones | 27

4.
Youth | 29
Girl on the beach | 30
Flame | 31
Grey shadow green | 32
Conjunctions | 33
A separating | 34
Abendigo's classmates | 36

5.
Scrooge applies for a posthumous posting | 38
Postcards | 39
Carousel: on the death of friends | 41
Brass | 42
True and false | 43
Ghosts in time | 44
Paper trails | 45

6.
Sidings | 48
Adam's daughter | 49
Storyteller | 50
The afterlife of Gulliver and Miss Havisham | 52
Alice next morning | 53
Space times | 54
Rag-picker | 55

7.
Arithmetic | 58
Unsettlement | 60
Noah at night | 61
Samarkand | 62
Familiars | 64
Peeling an orange | 65
They and us | 66

8.
Night thoughts | 69

Acknowledgments | 71

1.

These are an old man's words,
murmurings in traffic:
he's the figure at the crossroads,
watching sound,
listening to shadows:

Roots

In the second hour after midnight, the air
gathers moss, holding treelike
for half a quarantine, waiting for someone
to hear roots start to grow, and growing.

It is the time of ogres, when anything might happen,
even trust or terror, something nameless
with a shape you say you've almost seen,
through the narrow of an open door.

The ogres tell stories, of when they ruled the oceans,
when the shells began and the red tides: *Shade,*
they whisper, *shade,* cautioning

> *We had shadows once,*
> *and our shadows had shadows,*
> *then all our shadow's shadows*
> *lifted from the forest floor and*
> *splintered against the sun:*

In the silence-after,
if a tree-branch stutters, shatters, breaks,
you may see broken figures pass you by—

but in the second hour after midnight the moss
breathes, the tendrils that feed the forest
inch ahead, saying *Listen: It is not too soon—*

The cave painters knew: in their dark corners,
ambling in charcoal like elephants and arctic
bears, they saw their shadow's shadows eddying,

and wakening, *a scatter of almost light*:

they're telling you to find your other self,
the one who dreams in colour in the second hour,
who hears upheaval as the origin of laughter.

2.

juggling prepositions—
in, of, across, away—
shaking history's half-truths
for stories to live by: with, without,
accident, disorder:

On fields beside the moon

Walk briskly, for you walk on trouble:
history's unquiet here, the earth
pebbled with invention, music
grinning with discord

Walk firmly, for you walk on rumour:
the east wind coils, whips
sediment in strings, slings
whisper into shard

Blunders, barracking, bonding and want:
why do you expect any other stories?
you walk beside the moon: listen,
the dark, the laughter of rain

Harry's brothers

My mother loved reading stories, to her children
and herself, never losing her place: I think now
it was a way of coping, with the loss of her own
mother, the forced displacement, life in another
country, with aunts and uncles already at war:

she spoke often—whenever she spoke at all
about those years—of her eleven cousins, boys
she scarcely knew, ten of them killed in battle,
only the 9-year-old surviving, Harry his name—
I never heard what the rest had once been called:

or I've not remembered: it seems so long ago,
and distant, like a story in a language I didn't ever
learn—maybe one she didn't want to admit she knew,
or didn't want us to have to grapple with,
so read us Oz and animal tales instead, supposing

they would teach us happiness, a world where
everything stayed in its right place: not her fault
she kept looking for order, nor that she couldn't
stop the world from pitching, yet still I keep thinking
about what wasn't there: the absences,

the lost and missing, the hasn't-yet-been-found:
I learned distance from her, and distances, the anarchy
of authors whose stories wouldn't fix the world,
and gaps in the narrative of living
that wizards couldn't fill—

Cables

Like others at the age of four, I was frightened by
ambush: lions, tigers, crocodiles, bears, the wooden
clatter as escalator teeth snatched the slatted steps
beneath my feet and swallowed: *crunch, lurch*: battle-
cables snapping, looping into the dark: Oh yes, soon

we hunted explanations, ack-acking our way through
scrub and make-believe, hungry for secrets and stories—
but the uncles returning from overseas were silent:
a few strutted their ribbons, loud and cocksure, but
most wanted nothing more to do with guns, grenades,

the grinding down: *War*, they said, *you ate mud, and
mud ate you, and that's all you need to know.* So we
bound ourselves in colour and noise, dodged the gangs
of adolescent brass, and whirled through as much of
the rest of a life as was left on the edge of the wild.

I figured later that shadows pursued us all. Men
swaggering bark and rut just wanted to be told how
big they were, growling tiger-jawed to stage a private
fight against confusion. Even the silent uncles—
those who built ladders and lifted us up through

apple branches into plain words and resolutions—
had to keep on climbing through battle fatigue:
Maybe that's us too, now, holding the bears at bay,
trying to save ourselves and the ravelled earth
from the spinning teeth of an endless machine.

Fortune-tellers

By the time I was five I was already making up stories
to get my brother's attention—

I'd say we were going on a holiday (but weren't)
or getting a dog (because I wanted one)—

so you'd think I would have guessed when my brother
whispered that he knew guys named Gory Gus and
Desperate Ambrose (and that he'd tell me a secret
if I swore to shut up about it:

*school teachers told fortunes on Thursday afternoons . . .
they read tea leaves,* he said . . . *they could predict
the Irish Sweeps . . . their playing cards could tell
when the war would end*):

I crossed my heart (and hoped to die of course)—
and then repeated everything verbatim: now

I wonder why, but I think I wanted to explain the world
or at least hear that the world could be explained:

Why was news from the front so scarce? Why were
mothers so keen to hear anything, everything,
but upset every time an army letter arrived?

(What were they reading when they ran their fingers
over blacked-out spaces? What other words were hiding,
waiting to be seen?)

I know now that stories were a way of dealing
with what we didn't know and grappling
with what we couldn't be sure of:

Everyone needed answers, and maybe any truth
was welcome, even if only written in tea:

I was not the only story-teller then among my friends:
girls playing hopscotch were all predicting who
they would marry: boys bombarding each other with
mudballs and green apples were imagining their fathers:

and I was among them, roaming the bush
with willow sticks, inventing the brother I never had.

Filaments

We tell the same stories, weave the same web
of almost-true and never-quite-the-same

and call it memory or love or grief and happiness,
complications we know as brass and spiders, moss

and the needles of tamarack and pine:
we give shadows the name of tricksters, and rivers

the gift of beginning: what else do we need to know
except once and then, if and if only, only if and oranges—

water feeds us, earth lifts us, fire warms and air propels:
wagonwheels and after—we breathe stories

as though we invented them,
while in filament and land-shadow they imagine us—

Tin Box

The tin box opened one way only,
the lid hinged, loose-fitting, the colour
blue. And white. A Delft design.
Possibly it once held chocolates,
a gift perhaps, its romance something
only my parents remembered.

I knew it later—the box—and romance too,
but not together, or not at first, only
after the war, when I thought
I was beginning to understand.

I remember the box:
it sat on my father's workbench,
right beside the hammer, saw, the brace-and-
bit, all shipshape, cleaned and shelved,
ready for *next* and *needed*,
set aside for me.

Every evening I would head downstairs,
steal across the basement floor,
pick up the box and open it,
looking for windmills. The blue,
the white. Hearing a rush of gunfire,
pirates on the border, rattling anger,

danger. He'd set the box aside, my dad,
filling it with crossbones and cutlasses,
bolts and brackets, nickel-plated angle-irons,
bent brass and lost souls.

I turned invasion into story, story into time,
counted the nights I heard of one war,
and then two, and then another,
looking for what he'd lost, or set aside:
laughter perhaps, the hold
that tells of certainty and sea—

Ghosts

My father told stories that I utterly believed
but was never sure of: was it true that Uncle Thomas
died while felling a tree? why had I never met
Aunt Martha? what else could I maybe learn
about Cousin-Hattie-who-was-killed-by-lightning?

All three of them were real by the time
I went to school: I was absolute: I knew exactly
how tall the tree had grown, the axe's heft, the bit's
honed lip, the madness of Aunt Martha, Cousin
Hattie's rash dance with thunder. These were

my stories now, my claim on a history that dared
the wilderness and toyed with danger. Then
I forgot about them, played hide-and-seek instead
and soccer on a gravel field. Until later, when they
turned into ghosts. Restless, they loom at night,

even Aunt Martha, whom I know I invented: she's
the fiercest: adze, edge, eddy, the electric fury
at the heart of storm, she lives in the backlot of time,
where disappointment lies, playing with desire,
utopia and stone.

3.

speeding, idling, overtaking,
breakdown and budging in:
who drives, who cycles, who flies past:
narrating onward, still
asking why:

Pond ice

Red scarf, red mitts,
ice at the edge of pond water,
new skates hanging from the left hand:

Not yet, not yet, and yet just see if
just a test, only if, and then if only:
the mittens wet through:

How far before not at all,
that break between melt and
breathaway (the motherban)

Whisper, murmur, green ice
edging into later, escaping *I am* at last
bolting darting speeding streaking—

Wagon

When one of us got a metal wagon everyone
wanted to ride it all the way to the last stop
before Christmas: *does it go fast, how fast does
it go, does it go faster than Jimmy's wooden box,
can you steer it, can it fly,* and then Eddie sneered
do the wheels come off and that was it for a while.

Bright red paint. White lettering. *Radio Flyer.*
And yes it did go faster than the crate the others
carted to school with newsprint for the paper drive:
yes you could steer it, the wheels didn't wobble
on dicey axles and jam up just as you heaved it
to hilltop, and yes everyone did have a chance

to try it out as soon as Bobby's mother shouted
Take turns, you, and it lasted, chipped and rusted
by the time everyone was done, till Jimmy got a
bike and everyone argued about gears and speed
and yes Eddie sneered *can it fly* but this time yes
it could fly, faster than summer itself, the red

wagon, the paper drive at school, and even
Bobby's mother who it turned out had some illness
that others weren't supposed to know about or
talk about and didn't until after, when it was
already too late to say anything that made sense
except *she always wanted us to play fair*—

Biking with shadows

Wind tugging breathing—biking over into
shadow—bucket thistle-funnel-dragon breathing
narrowgauge and spinning—spokes

snow leaning water solid
vanishing in funnel ferris-
wheeling amberwinging dragonthistle turning
heeling now whirling under-
                    wafer-water
colour umber-runner reeling—fire weeding
fire ferris cycle double shadow water
wheeling doublevision spinning open air in
open air the after air the umberdragon amberair
the breathing in the breathing in the breathing in

        shadow

the breathing in

Flood

The waters rise,

earth gives way
at the edges,
learns
for a fraction of time
to swim,

the algebra
of space—

The cost of land

Guy in a gold convertible stops, hands out tracts,
shouts *Do I have a deal for you sure thing so help me*
God nothin' to lose your horse is old I see and lame
I'll give you twenny save you from lookin' anywheres
else that rain that's comin' won't be stoppin' any time
soon so whaddoya say?

Two acres done, the solitary man on the John Deere
fastens on the furrows behind him, secretly gleeful
that nothing is out of line, but unsmiling (fearing pride),
certain his gods are intractable: daily they withhold
the rain, batter him with fire and promises, his time
is short, he knows he still has far more fields to clear—

The thresher next, in the horse-drawn field,
watches the western sky for rain and strangers:
Dark, he murmurs, muscles taut, *nothing is*
not nothing: goes quiet inside the old rules,
a fallow field's alive with signs
and nothing, tense, distracts him—

The field

Some called the field fallow, saying *winter wheat*
as though that explained an emptiness:

the children knew better—finding a magic field
where chickweed and curly dock were already
spreading rumour, unearthing stones:

small trees were growing there with animal dens
in the hollows, foxtail and horsetail, crabgrass and
lamb's quarters, amaranth and shepherds' purse:

and there they play, finding stellar treasure, shadow
danger, sailors' messages and dandelion gold:

the adults warn *Be wary* and *Yes* the children say
and are, scavenger hunts among the willows, races
through the nettles, tag wherever open spaces beckon:

Meet you in the field, they say, whole generations
gambolling, the dry stalks giving way to bees:

Some grown-ups trip on dodder and bindweed, thistle
and vetch, the field growing over them like buckthorn:
but those who still listen as children do will hear

tales from an open ground, of a summer being happy,
together, swimming through the weeds:

Riverstones

The five of them know the way, they
race through bush to the canyon's edge leap
over and down, winding, alive, past edge and ledge
till the last of the leaning alders tips
into the eddies, the river bends west and distance
hurtles out of hearing, the riverstones rushing—

flinging off sunsweat and jeans and tees and
colour and—branch-slapping black thorn—they are
furrows in time, creasing the air they do not see,
no mind now for age or for after, speeding,
naked and skinny and into the cold—immersing

immune to sunblister, ice—they're part of the river,
buoyant with joy, the cold is their friend,
the riverstones laughing, and all that they are
is down the hill under-and-over outside—

danger, they say, they know from before, yes
glass, rip, slick stones the whirlpool,
the river still running as long as they're here—

when trips, when tumbles, the edge over under
emerging that day when the riverstones rolled

and the four of them remember—

4.

dangerous,
this place of passing:
recognizing:
even together
we are apart:

Youth

In an apple orchard in another time,
stripped to summer stippled brown,
I was free from the punishment of skin—
high on a hillside, I rambled in wanting,
revelled in being—

I did not call it happiness, I knew it was,
the day was I and I the day
and all and everything around was singing—

Seven swallows tilting the mountain,
cider press and cleft of haystack,
prick of blackberry bush and motion motion,
what do they tell us now of fluttertouch
the waterfall of joy—

Lips cheeks belly button romance, hayrick
wracked and roadside sparrowgrass, stalks
of timothy gone to sand:
when did we become our fathers?

Before the Inca in the continent's far desert,
the Nazca drew berrylines to tell the time that
was, human heron hummingbird
for stars and sky to see, singing then,
like ladders into apple trees,
watersongs to the supple sun—

Girl on the beach

She walked on the beach every weekend   we
saw her   we stopped building sandcastles and
watching the tide roll in   we said we no longer
cared when the moats filled and the turrets fell

She walked on the beach   along the dry edges
where winter had abandoned kelp and empty
clamshells and in the periwinkle zone of inter-
tide or in the ocean shallows where small fish

darted and children-with-parents played   She
walked on the beach we said waiting or wanting
and we said yes but not yet aloud   and she
walked alone on the beach alone and wanted

being alone   The whole summer long she walked
and we saw her   She walked and we saw her
walking   then and the weekend after and then
in the waves and we imagined   the wind

Flame

Street traffic's bunching, bucking, buckling:
appointments, payments, missed and over-
due, lost letters hunger and need—

a siren blares, abrupt as pinnacles,
pedestrians turn—

Is it me, Is it close, Is it anyone I know ...
as though a flick of the head
will staunch the tide.

A captain glances shorewards, looking
for a lighthouse flashing, does he see reeds
pulsing him home, does he hear strange music
and the shuffle of the orange trees?

I know the answer to this riddle,
says the grey man on the corner, signing mute,
begging for breakfast and beer.

Lights flash. Flames ripple.
Heads twisting, checking the heat
in a plate glass window.

Grey shadow green

I can picture their faces, hear their sudden laughter,
catch a moment when they burst forward, back away,
blush or glower, bite their lips or grin: their images
are clear, I carry them with me, each alone,
though in the dark they now begin to blur

The girl I had a Friday crush on,
who wasn't there on Monday:
alas, authorities said, there was an accident

The favourite aunt who whispered *Go, Do not
wait for me*, and went: The April friend hollering
See you in September, who overturned in summer
(a narrow storm): Young woman, old man,
one lasting only till her child was born, the other
writing *I have a small problem to deal with: silence*

And one old woman who didn't remember who I was
but always offered tea:
she's not coming back this time I asked, is she,
and no she wasn't

Though they all do, sometimes:
perfume will remind me, or a colour,
maybe cherry pink, canary yellow,
or some muted hue like sparrowgrass
in the wake of hunter green:

Conjunctions

Grammar is the route a story takes
from where you stand to where
you only think you want to go:

down the slide of *if,* around the endless
loop of *and,* through a break in the wall of *but,*
or (*or,* a forked road) along the corrugated
cobblestones that pave an alleyway of *though,
although, except that, provided*:

maybe you'll find you've been circling a cloverleaf
for hours *when, as soon as, not yet, by the time that,
till, until, whenever,* but (there it is again) a rope
ladder of *because* insists on asking where you
really think you're going, who you're listening to,
and why, and you climb (or slip, or swing):

story follows its own rules: you may think
you're on a cablecar to snowfields, *so* (a sail, a sail,
a parasail) who have you readied yourself to meet
(conjunctions)
when your narrative turns (the wagon road
is rougher than you think, the old horse lame)
to dare the dark and meet the sea—

A separating

Spring gardens stretch to the outside ends of time—tulip and jonquil nurseries boasting kingsize beds of colour: parrot, plain, butterfly pied.

Hand in hand, onlookers glance up and drift on, certain they're looking wise—until the botanist happens by, murmuring *Narcissus, every one.*

In coming months the flowers fade, the drying out begins: bulbs lifted, bulblets set aside (in-case-they-may-be-sorted-one-day: listed, labelled, sold). Not easy, this. Promises are made, some kept, some buried. *Ifs and ands. Next year's a gamble. Ill winds, late frosts. Spider mites and aphids.* (The botanist mutters so many old wives' tales, you can almost hear the knitting needles: *Work for spring, prepare for fall.*)

Overwinter and under cover: planters learn to reckon fallow-times, but drawn-out ice surprises even them. The botanist writes a guide: it hums with the usual bees: *What can grow here isn't always what will.* (Does anyone read? The tulips know. Weeds spread.)

If summer ever does come back, the arboretum will open its gates to parents, neighbours, lovers, brothers, in-laws, pets, and second cousins: the botanist hears them chatter contradictions through the groves, the brakes, the spinneys: *The garden looks so natural, looks enchanted, looks as though it's always been here.*

Hard work, the botanist mutters to no-one in particular, *keeping it all together*—as if patching a broken fence could save the monarch butterflies. *Sometimes they last,* he adds, under his breath, *and sometimes they don't, or don't come back.* (*Sometimes you look at the sky and just hope for milkweed.*)

(Others whisper they can already catch the scent of afterwards, *they knew it would happen, the crop would fail.* At the edge of order, they say, they can hear the slow rumble of the wild plums.)

Abendigo's classmates

Yeah, we talk about the old days, the two years at college,
and every now and then someone mentions Shadrach—
I think there were three of them altogether—the third one
always said I got his name wrong, but I could never
tell the difference.

Anyway, that's a long time ago, and mostly I remember
spending hours on dinosaur stuff like the right size of chisels
instead of anything fun. Not that we had many options.
Thinking out loud got you a long day in a bonfire.
Or a short date with the big cats.

Some choice.

Who could blame us for sitting back and doing nothing?
Turns out everyone could—especially after those three
made a name for themselves,
getting up the nose of the guys in charge—

wasn't long of course before they got picked up
and shut away—but they managed to survive somehow,
got promoted, shone. That's the short version,
the one we talk about.

Me and my crew, we figure there's another story there,
if anyone can ever tell it proper like. One that
leaves out the smoke and the sweet-talk
and the stale jokes.

Might explain why we're still talking.

5.

hoops and circuses, roundabouts
and empty rings:
stories he keeps coming back to:
stories that all along
have been riding with him:

Scrooge applies for a posthumous posting

To: Nezer.com   From: Ghostbank Central, Inc.
Dear sir/madam, may I call you ebenezer thank you for your query our lines are unusually busy wait time may be over fourteen hours our agent will reach you asap with preliminary questions fyi please note current openings in our haunts division require air travel which has been simplified for registered ghosts successful applicants will be stationed overseas where holiday surges of gimcrack sellers tawdry painters saccharine greeters jarring warblers have pumped the demand for fresh haunters if these opportunities suit your needs leave a detailed curriculum vitae with ms marley at reception for further information push button 4 phantom vacuums standard wraiths and quivering spectres need not apply

Postcards

Steam—
billowing—
looking picturesque: but as you've left home once, twice,
maybe more, you know old trains up close,
oily puddles by the track, acrid clouds of exhaust,
soot in the nostrils, grime on a linen handkerchief—
(do you just write *pretty peaceful*—or say what once passed
for daring, early on—penny on a tram rail, how you laughed
at rattle-distorted-heads-and-tails
then joined in the classroom singalong *God Save,
Maple Forever,* trusting in the likelihood—was it real,
or already rebellion, shadow resistance, undeclared romance:

until inland, halfway across the country, when you thought
you had found connection)—HAND CAR BUD CAR COAL
CAR FREIGHT CAR BAGGAGE CAR BOX CAR DOME CAR OLD
ENGINE DIESEL ELECTRIC, RED CABOOSE—
clumsy bunks, sleeping aboard *The Canadian*
(the porter's kindness):

awkward, the dining car ballet, elegance unfamiliar, then patched,
then discontinued—did they pass for politics, those days and days
aboard the continent—coupling, uncoupling, humid summer heat,
ice drawing outside in, horns echoing railway, *railway*:
churn thunder rumble screech sway—winter smoke and steam—

picture heartbeat: the motion of being aboard—the rhythms
steady until they aren't: lurch at a crossing—split in the

tracks—
who do you write to now? hiss hot easing cooling shunting:
release: will you get back on, settle,
or risk being left on the siding—

Carousel: on the death of friends

Rooting around in the back alleys of grief,
kicking lamentation aside, petulant
even after anger fails, still spitting spleen
and seething ... *where is joy?* Joy is slow,

late coming home from the dusty carousel,
trudging rutted paths and riding uncoupled
the chipped horses, hungry: How did the
Cavaliers cope with pestilence and plague?

How did the friends of Piltdown Man deal with
losing him—in fire, water, quill and chalk?
picturing the great hunt then, pairing exodus
with laughter now: inventing image. Survivors'

genes are those that feed our bodies: they paint
the herds of wild elephants we tracked through
hot forests, rearrange the crawl of pubs where
starched collars frayed: we are and are not them—

sharing a place, inheriting a time, we
inhabit connection: how this longing bonds us,
intensity sustains: through club and cave,
and all the ragged distances of fairground.

Brass

Walk softly in the nave: you're treading on history here,
you don't want to ruffle the ghosts—the knights
and ladies and local squires who lie beneath the footworn
flagstones, or the country centuries of pale parishioners
who haunt the tilted crosses in the chapel graveyard:

walk carefully: the North is cold, the winter damp,
the dominie's seen people like you before, bending
to the flat brass plates in the aisle—still here from when
knights were young and ladies wore fierce headbands
and patterned kirtles—you may be offered free advice
or a knitted shawl, but you're the stranger here,

kneel caringly, the ghosts are watching from behind
the rood screen, whispering as you take heelball to paper
and trace the figures on the brass engravings: be wary,
you may think the knight is bandy-legged, the lady haughty,
the brash squire self-important, but say nothing, centuries
of choirboys have said worse, and you're here to admire
the remnants of time not referee the congregation:

rise cautiously, you're not used to bending—perhaps you
should think twice before you step into the next nave,
badger the next brass, interrupt the next cloisters
and the long goodbyes of elder, ash, and yew.

True and false

My mother saw the *Titanic* sink, my mother
heard that the ship had sunk, my mother sailed
the Atlantic the year the *Titanic* sank with John
Jacob Astor: one of these is true, one almost true,
one maybe a way to tell a different loss, a tale
of distance, absence, apple trees and pandemonium:
I may never know the whole truth:

she added more to the story of the White Star Line,
lost every time she told it: we sat enthralled,
seeing the iceberg loom from the north, hearing
the frozen crack against intemperate steel and the
cries of those who perished and those who survived:
smelling the salt air, the codfish gambolling with
Lady Astor's diamonds, watching the iceberg win:

my mother was nine when she was sent away—
about the same age her children were when decades on
she started telling us her tale: in that version Lady Astor
was on a different deck, no one saw the diamonds
or mentioned the cod: my mother's ship had already
docked and her life in another country just about
to begin: we heard about the ice later, and the war:

the first war: and read *Anne of Green Gables* as well,
and Aesop's *Fables*, and mixed them up with tales
of sailing ships and Kipling's *Kim*: what else was there
to do on the farm, besides field work and making do:
and the fighting: some of it inside: her stories told us
of the Ocean Deep, but we never fathomed just how
true that was, how cold the story made her feel:

Ghosts in time

You see them, and then they're gone—names
you used to know and now can't call to mind,
faces dimmer than they used to be—*that one
looks like Adam's boy or was it the Baptist's
daughter*—facts uttered with firm uncertainty—
*something about the eyes, but different,
I think it's the way they're looking past you
all the time*—like strangers crossing the other way
at a busy corner, only half seen, or half seeing,
intent on some important thing they still think
they need to know—and they do, need to know
I mean, for a while yet, though they too will find
one day that the ghosts are firmer than before
and appear more often and you hold them close—

Paper trails

The front room
was where we kept the chairs we never sat in.
The ones for Company.

The back room was for kettles of soup: it's where we ate
and where we swept up all the sawdust trails
that spilled like fingerprints
when the hopper was almost empty.

I kept to myself, I learned the rules,
and when it came my turn to fetch a bucket
to feed the kitchen stove, I learned those rules as well:
<u>don't fill to the brim, fill to *almost*,</u>
<u>and don't trail smithereens the whole way after.</u>

Always, there was *after*.

I could read by the time I saw the war map
that granddad had tacked to the wood storage wall—
but I couldn't yet translate its signs,
not till he told me the map was tracking battle sites
and torn fronts: (((((> > > > >

I'd seen the marks—
but I read them as hills and mountains, drew them
in purple wax and green, imagined secret codes
so I could pass unruly into strangers' hideaways:

After, I saw raw bones and spilled blood,
cold fires and wind-swept wreckage.

I've gone back often, into uniformed disorder
and the almost past. I write messages on stone
to people I scarcely knew.   ( )   ( )   ( )
I see dust.
              And sometimes, in winter,
I look for rough trails off the map,
and I follow them as far as they will let me
into the crayon mountains.

6.

*naming nouns: presence, absence,
the spaces between, abstract,
concrete, horns and scrapes
and passages and ties: laughter
tumbling, fidgeting regrets:*

Sidings

The children say *Your stories all start with a missing
line*—I know: because I know the train shrieks past me
every summer dark, telling the riverside to make way,
'the Kettle Valley doesn't run there any more' I say:
electric's coming through:

*

Aboard the silence of the TGV, I feel the coal-fired
hiss of steam that cuffs winter days along the Thames
and Aire and Ouse—stagger by the sidings of an Avon
yard, the earth freezing, underbuckling Now
and shunting me aside:

*

Même sur la rive gauche, seeing a couple curling
in a corner out of Dubuffet, I sip tisane, hear phantom
jazz, touch the thumbed edges of a ragged menu,
smell the scented bark of the peeling plane tree:

*

rail lines into things past, grey ties at the edge of lonely,
shadows in delight:

one day I hope the children too will stumble across a line,
hear music spiking on an odyssey of absence,

find longhand notes on aging paper, branches
that tell them strange how much they're loved.

Adam's daughter

Every day, I see her turn her head
towards the lemon tree in the upper garden:
every day she slips closer,
climbing the seven stairs the gardener's carved
in old limestone,
taking one step, two, until the branches dance for her
and she embraces them, whispering.

Once there was a time when she drew
chalk lines on the terraces and leapt the edges,
counting millipedes and marvels, all as one,
but now she drifts from clay to ever after,
the tree embraces her.

She knows her mind, the gardener sighs,
and signs to me that he can hear them singing,
though I, who hear nothing now,
can only touch the distances and grieve.

One day she will be gone, he says.
I ask why, but then already know.
The lemons ripen daily,
the branches hang low,
and I remember other arms, old hopping stones,
and that sweet sharp tang.

Storyteller

The carrots weeded themselves, the storyteller murmurs, saying what he believes is true—*Nothing in my father's garden sprouted—lettuce heads arranged the beets, five separate kernels hilled each other, overnight the rows appeared and celery stalks grew up outside the rim of random*:

he lies of course—secretly he knows how much his father sweated worries into sequence:

on his own now he's teasing glimpses into memorized lines, thinking he's in control: but the story's not his: in the pit the groundlings know that words are runner beans and thorns: they tell their own tales—fungus to fallow, seedtime to reaping,

it's the unpredictables that scratch and scramble the seasons' play—what else could coax sticks into dragonseed, morph pebbles into knobbled knees, stroke grandmother trees to bleed intentions into the gravel grounds:

you think I'm wrong? listen to the storyteller's words—his narratives are onion-tales, shadows inside shadows, the after-story smoke that plumes in an autumn burning: they're the ogres terrors giant trolls erratic ghouls and bogeymen that dislocate us: why else would we keep asking *what-happened-then* about some strangeness that hasn't happened yet:

it's the patch of thorns we keep looking for, the love and fear that coiled inside the father's garden even though he never said (who are the drifters who've grown beside you as you've wandered into *Darwin/Dickens/desire/Defoe* (and kept on lurking after the gates were closed (they're monsters you say, and you love them—

your story begins even before you've seen them, before you
even know they're there and always after, when they wrinkle
out of the shadows and stop you on the way to Samarkand
or the sweating oil ponds: do you hear the shouting from
the pit? raspberries, laughter, heckling, haze:

it prompts you: the stories you think you're telling were
already staging you: why have you not yet figured out that
the ground's unstable, the garden you say you're looking for
has never fostered order: can you tell you're painting smoke?
yes—and smoke tells stories too, once-upon-a-fire and a
row of flames—

The afterlife of Gulliver and Miss Havisham

Yes, we know what happened—he got trampled
by his idea of Horse and she went up in flames,
it wasn't pretty. But after—can we even imagine
after? Maybe she travelled abroad and he built a
country house, though likely not much changed.
Maybe they traded stories over oatcakes and tea
in the raspberry drawing room. Or simply
retreated into id and ego, clinging to powdered
wigs and brass cargo hooks, unaware that
theirs was a dying art. So many are like them,
previous and stubborn—blurring mind and manners,
replaying the tight stamp of silence, rehearsing
the unstable politics of dissatisfaction.

Alice next morning

Promises, *hah!* I doubt my friends would actually get it—
what happened with the dormouse I mean, or the hours
I spent drinking tea with a rabbit—not after I'd been griping
so much about that glossy magazine shoot and what it

said about young women, and old ones too, each of them
sweaty and hot, lugging sixty pounds of fresh tea-leaves
up and down a bluff-side every day but all smiley-smiley
when some guy comes along and takes their picture—

and for what? A promise, a basket, a flat hat, a dash
of Darjeeling? Has me asking a lot about last night—
What was I thinking, going out in the rain like that
with a crazy man and whatever that rabbit put in the tea.

Supposed to be re-*freshing*, right? So today I'm looking
for difference. But all I see are the same old hats, hear
the same fast talk about *intemperate* weather, smell
the same stale *cross-my-heart* promises: so who's to say

what's ordinary and what's not—unless that gunfire's real
and tall buildings are falling because a preacher's gone mad
or a slithering bonehead's spiked a drink or a hifalutin
mega-wig has gobbled the dormice and swallowed the air—

Space times

In 1942 I daily spread the comics on the floor—
the paper's pinched panels all in black-and-white—
but on the sixth day the comics turned up supersized:
the printers said *Let there be colour*—Tarzan, Mandrake,
the Pirates, Flash Gordon—on Saturdays we knew
that good knights won every tournament, war would be
over quickly, the wildwood secure.

In 2022 a tv interviewer asks an expert
what to expect from Artemis One,
the rocket that carries mannikins to the moon—

Hunting the other side, he says, *we'll witness a new world
being born*: he's excited, as though he can already
see through darkness, face to face—

Next time, he adds, *with Artemis Two,
we'll put three people on board,
and a Canadian,
and a woman:
one of them will be coloured.*

He doesn't say *Let X denote live astronauts*
or seem to know his story draws boxes,
a geometry of precedence and power—
space is limited perhaps, and time short:

Later, his panel will rise to say their own names.

The nightly wars that no-one mentions keep thundering on.

Rag-picker

When the rain mutters *after-summer*,
when the kid next door moves away,
when the next kid's a bully, the father is working
or not working or maybe not even there this year
and the mother says Go play,

as if it matters, as if it's possible, as if at last it's real,
you know it's fall, and there you stay

until the junkman's wooden wagon thunders by:
the one that rolls noise out of nowhere, lifts you off the cracked
cement and rushes you up through an ink-berry grey,
above the rain and into the hollow that's under the weeping:

only the wagon knows you here,
follows the heave to the willow tree:
only the wagon hears you saying rags and thistles, lies and bones,
and there you stay

until the wagon rumbles,
jars and jangles and rattles and whirs, jolts and hums and
thrums and stirs, and the second time it flies, you choose
inarush to carry you back

to nowhere somewhere others and soon, hearing why and
where-did-you-go and let's climb the junkwagon
one more time,
ride into rhyme and over the rain,
and see if we can laugh

the way we used to laugh, remembering summers that never began—

7.

how much he loves the skewed world—
because it's always being retold,
storytelling calling Time:
silence, and then
drive:

Arithmetic

In elementary school our teacher told us facts to give us
places in the world: our place was called Vancouver, and
also Canada, our king was called King George and every day
we sang a song to make him glorious and happy, and we
repeated these facts until they sounded real and we were
happy then, for then we also had names and seemed real:
we didn't know yet our names were only partly true, our
rocky country shared, our place at war, our laughter like our
happiness uncertain, brittle, rough, and elementary, insecure:

In elementary school our teachers said our city and the
point of land on which our city stood had many names
although we called it as we did (our teachers said) because
of Captain George Vancouver of King George's ship *Discovery*,
who discovered here and also named the sounds and straits
and boulevards and passages that marked our places
in the world, and we repeated these names as though
he'd found us too: because we didn't know yet that facts
like these were angular and only partly true (all of us

and those who came before were living in parentheses):
In elementary school we learned about tracks and rocks and
lighthouse points: we learned that Captain George had named
them too, but for his friends, whose names were Brockton
Atkinson and Grey, and we, the teachers said, we were at war,
again they said, but white lighthouses flashed to sea, so we
could run the track at Brockton Oval, gawk at the stunted tree

on Siwash Rock, stagger at giant evergreens by Atkinson, and
settle safely on the cliffs at Grey and watch the red sun set:

In elementary school we learned only some of the things
the teachers told us: we were happy, we began to say, but
not always: our place was glorious, but we didn't play outside
when sirens warned of dangerfog and blackout: we learned
unfair and words the teachers called forbidden but didn't yet
fathom multiplication tables, smallpox, or stunted lives:
In the forest at a distance close to Brockton, maybe some
of us saw the last people living at WhoiWhoi: we didn't know
they were the last: although we saw the dark close in, we didn't

stick around to ask or pause in place to learn more, and Captain
George didn't have a name for where they lived or any true fact
for who they were: he didn't see the villages he sailed past:
he didn't name Ulksen, or Skaywitsut, or Whoi Whoi, or Snauq,
or else ignored them: maybe he saw an absence he didn't wish
to name or thought the people in place already always here
didn't altogether count: maybe he couldn't hear the syllables
of Halkomelem languages (səṅaʔqʷ and χʷayχ̇ʷəy̓) or just decided
not to listen to ancestral stories, place and custom, but map

the Empire's acres, count the spars and shoals and let
c̓əsnaʔəm and sɬχiləx disappear: In elementary school,
when teachers called our names, we answered *here* and
learned to count to ten: they were right about some things,
our teachers, and wrong about others, and so were we:
we mastered printing, drawing, plus and minus signs, x's,
goes-into's, and how to spell *arithmetic*: we didn't know yet
that spelling X would come to mean unknown, the Great
Divide site a rocky trench, pointed words map a sentence,
absence prove a sign of long division:

Unsettlement

You wake up and you've been living in some town
on the Silk Road a thousand years ago maybe Tash-
kent or Samarkand a place where afternoon was kind
and rain was gentle and you and the old dog you loved
as a child were playing frisbee until the dog ran away
and then farther away the frisbee fell to earth and you
now don't remember where you'd been or the message you
know you had to carry from wherever then to where you
are now and someone everyone it seems is blaming you
and you're racing through some string of things you
don't want to hear now things you did that still haunt you
things you didn't do that haunt you even more some
hushed-up whispers scents signs shivering scenes
ghost words you said or didn't say some hurt you felt or
fed and *Why* you ask and *Why* and *Why* because of pain
you say because of joy and slowly start remembering
time because you love and play and live and err and
settle slowly into sun the morning sun the silken rain

Noah at night

I remember
I used to remember
names, dates,
how soon and then after:
the demitasses of microtime.

Before the flood.

Now is only
a nomad crocodile
thrashing away on empty nights
outside the upstairs window.

I feel the whisk of curtains,
hear the angle of the wary light
alter,
      murmur *when*
and find deep shade where thyme
and rosemary
used to furrow the afternoon:

Lagooned:

Now the crocodile comes,
swallowing whole
old crocks of syllables,
to see who answers,
besides the moon—

Samarkand

The photographs on the wall have begun to talk to me,
aloud, Aunt Josephine severe, a dust mop in her hand,
Uncle Wilbur with a shovel, the greats and grands
and cousins-long-removed all nudging to get a word in:
what is it with you people, why can't you ever
let anything go, old mud spots, old rivalries, old
tin can labels for a scrapbook page—*Begone*, I say,
like Hamlet, Henry, Othello, *Get thee away, avaunt*—
though none respond: relics they are,
of teatimes and parasols, pretty maids all in a row,
Go hence and not return! I see judgment, I see love,
I see chocolate in a baseball glove: why do I bring back
fragments, why do I remember at all, what use is history
except to celebrate loss and regret what's still to come?

The old ones talk of Samarkand as though they lived there,
a dream of purple turrets, perfumed silk, and magic stallions.

Nay. But who says Nay any more, except for horses? Nay,
nay, nay: Aunt Josephine, please smile for once, and
Wilbur, dig that hole as deep as you damn well want to,
you have my blessing, and all those promising infants that
turned into me, you too, just relax: the future you have in
store will be one you can wrestle with, it'll just not be
the one you thought was promised: so be it: you'll deal with it,
you'll find it fascinating, disruptive, outrageous, beautiful,
stop spilling your milk and get on with eating your cereal,
I know I know, it's dry and tasteless, but what you're trying
to write? Oh, that's amazing: it's called life, don't be afraid,
and don't wait: it's just around the corner, not yet framed—

It won't be the Samarkand of old men's verses, but it'll be something else, and that's all you need to keep going. On.

Familiars

Past deadfall and slide,
through the round haze of distance
the old man scrambles, minding each slow step
from now to long before:

Height is his friend, he says,
pausing on the next outcrop, or the last, shadow's
rumpled fold, darkness the music of his pale familiars:

He talks with them, the gods he hears
in these old altitudes, the hemlocks pulsing, frond and
fungus all *a tempo*, bark and lichen branch and berry
ring by ring—

friends who know the long climb, the hard
descent, the lost and open spaces in between—

> if you were here,
> if you could listen with me,
> if you'd answer, if you'd
>   see say tell—

hours counting the stones,
cougar in his ears, black bear, cuffed cub,
spotted fawn's curled shiver in the sedges—
always aware of *if*:

> if you could listen you would already know
> the song the needles sing
>   *alive, I am, we are alive—*

Peeling an orange

At a Christmas party once,
in the midst of a bitter war,
an army captain gave me an orange:

Everything else that day was dun-coloured:
khaki uniforms and plaited straw, chipped mugs
on trestle tables—bare bites of time—
even the crepe paper streamers hanging
limp from the rafters
looked already dead:

Go play with the other childr en, my mother urges me,
Be on your best behaviour—her message mixed:
I'd learned that speech was risky, only silence safe—

So I sat apart, watching the soldiers wheel and turn
and the afternoon unfold like cut-outs: someone
singing *Deck the Halls,* someone *Men of Harlech,*
young woman high on hope, old fellow deep in ale:
I was trying to figure out the masks that people wore,
and read the fragile truce between tart and crude:

When I took the orange from the bearded captain,
I peeled it slowly, tracking for the first time
the strange sour sweet of citrus:

Now that another war has started, I see him again,
wandering the orchards of my paper-chain imagination,
teaching me to strip away the ragged bitter rind
and once more savour what's to come—

They and us

Everything started with the war:

Before it began They said we had to live for After
and so we tried parcelling food and collecting string
and cancelling the light:
                       but there were trees,
and so we looked for laughter and invented play:

and then They said *be quiet* and cut down all the trees,
so we invented birds and listened to the rooftops
and the air singing on its own
                       until They cancelled music
and the colour green,
        and we tried to invent orcas in the water
        but already both were disappearing :

Before the war began They promised After,
but After never quite began
        because no one forgot the During,
and that was good because we needed to remember
and that was bad because we needed
        to clear away the dust and find the little people,
and that's when They said we needed plastic ice cream
and new bombs to try, to see if they'd taste the same,
and when they did or when they didn't They said it
didn't matter,
        giving us explanations that sounded
        like the old rumours that we'd heard before
        and all the homework that we said the dog
        had eaten but we knew was never real:

and when the air thinned and water stopped flowing,
we tried to tell a different story, but it was late, and
now They said we had to stop speaking and live for
artifice instead, dodge and gambit, racket ruse and bland:

They cancelled stories, calling any hurt a flag,
anxiety a competition: mapping affront in the dark
and talking war again:

and we lost the chance to hear the orcas up close
and the channels of the ocean flowing green:

but at the edges of the last earth we're still here,
with string and light and riverrun,
reinventing some of the stories that we used to hear
and rooting in the margins for a living tree:

8.

gathering the afterwords:
age he didn't understand until he got there,
youth he couldn't ever let go:
in reverse and inching forward,
reinventing now:

Night thoughts

Now is the time for stars, the moon dark
and distance falling away: in a black sky
they beckon—or warn—glittering illusion
or nebulous promise: origins and after:

*

Look up: see how light tries to touch us,
and how it falters, galaxies in their last throes
shining, percussion flame and stone: shadow's
the certainty we tenant by day, stone
the anxious craving we carry into the dark:

*

Now is the time to name the stars as the old ones did,
for mourning and healing, sacrifice and fear: night
is the time for the stars to sign: see what they tell us
of love and dying: Andromeda's on fire, the great bear
lost in space:

*

I dawdle at the edge of reason, wondering *what if*
and *if only* with a confidence I no longer share: Now
is a depth of dark we read as end-time: beauty, desire,
ecstasy, pain—knowing, however loudly we trumpet belief
or what we say is true, that we hold uncertainty in our hands
like rain: our time is now, we say, watching it flash and
flicker,
slip away:

*

Night is a time to remember the stars,
see dark beginning and darkness burning:
when is the time to remember now:

*

Shine, shimmer, fade: looking up, are we looking away,
fixing future in the origins of time: and are we
in the same time trying to find where we ourselves began:

*

Now is the night to remember ourselves:
the constellations we claim as ancestry: codes
of choice and hidden bargain, spaces in the night
where we look for before, ghosts of the past
as well as shadows of the stars:

*

Imagining the first burn, the first light in the first dark:
imagining the first Neanderthals gathering by riverbank
to decipher the night: was it their genes that gave us
muscle and the need now to look for meaning in the stars:

*

Now is the time to spell the ghosts and drum away despair:
look into the dark, sing morning again, and reach across
the burning distances:

Acknowledgments

I am indebted to friends and family for their patience while this book came into being: especially to Ron Smith, who over the space of a single year read these poems one by one (and more besides), commenting on each; together with Pat Smith, he helped me listen for cadence, sort out what needed to be added (and set aside what needed to be dropped). André Gérard shared ideas about poetry with me and listened while I struggled to explain why Samarkand kept reappearing in these lines. David Stover, at Rock's Mills Press, encouraged me as I was revising the text. Thank you to them all for their care and their encouragement.

I want also to express my gratitude to several print and online guides to Halkomelem languages, including Wayne Suttles' *Musqueam Reference Grammar* (Vancouver: UBC Press, 2004); and two websites, https://www.musqueam.bc.ca/departments/community-services/language [for information on Musqueam [xʷməθkʷəy̓əm] words and pronunciation]; and https://www.kwiawtstelmexw.com/language-resources [for information on the Squamish language]. 'Siwash Rock' (alluded to in 'Arithmetic') is the Chinook (trade jargon) name still used to refer to a familiar 'sea stack' or offshore rock outcrop in Vancouver's Stanley Park. Indigenous peoples refer to it as a 'transformation stone'—the Musqueam name for the rock is Sḻx̱iləx, meaning 'the Standing One,' and the Squamish name is Slhx̱i7lsh, meaning 'Standing Man.'

Special thanks also go to Karen New, who read the entire series of poems and—appreciating the contexts within which they were written—generously helped transform them into an ordered sequence; and to Peter New, whose sense of theatre and love of laughter helped feed the tempo of the book, contributing immeasurably to the balance between history and memory, anecdote and life. I thank Peter also for the photograph of the painting that is pictured on the book's cover. Above all, I thank Peggy New, as always, for her counsel, encouragement, insights into the language of poetry, and constant love.

About the Author

William New was born in 1938 in Vancouver, British Columbia, the city where he currently lives. A graduate of the University of British Columbia and the University of Leeds, and a prize-winning teacher and writer, he taught at UBC for almost four decades. During this time he edited the journal *Canadian Literature* for seventeen years and taught a range of literary courses, focussing on Canada and the Commonwealth. Author and editor of some fifty books and several scores of essays and reviews, he was awarded the Royal Society of Canada's Lorne Pierce Medal in 2004. For his services to creative and critical writing he was named an Officer of the Order of Canada in 2006.

His books of history and literary commentary range from *Articulating West* (1972) to *Land Sliding* (1997), *A History of Canadian Literature* (2nd ed., 2003), and several studies of poetry, the short story, irony, and postcolonial narrative, as in *Dreams of Speech and Violence* (1987) and *Reading Mansfield and Metaphors of Form* (1999). Editor of the *Encyclopedia of Literature in Canada* (2002), he has also studied how the personal and the local affect political attitudes, as in *Borderlands* (1998) and *Grandchild of Empire* (2003).

William New's creative works include five books for children, from *Vanilla Gorilla* (1998) to the internationally honoured *The Year I Was Grounded* (2008); and his poetry collections range from *Science Lessons* (1996) to *Underwood Log* (2004, shortlisted for the Governor General's Award), *YVR* (2011, winner of the City of Vancouver Award), *Neighbours* (2017), and *In the Plague Year* (2021).

www.ingramcontent.com/pod-product-compliance
Lightning Source LLC
Chambersburg PA
CBHW060411080526
44583CB00012B/533